# Sketching

## with

RAY
EVANS

First published in 1989
by William Collins Sons & Co., Ltd
London · Glasgow · Sydney
Auckland · Toronto · Johannesburg

**British Library Cataloguing in Publication
Data**
Evans, Ray, 1920–
    Sketching with Ray Evans – (Sketching with
    artists).
    1. Sketch. Manuals
    I. Title  II. Series

ISBN 0 00 412307 7

*Art editor: Caroline Hill*
*Designer: Monica Chia*
Filmset by Ace Filmsetting Ltd, Frome,
Somerset
Colour reproduction by Bright Arts,
Hong Kong
Printed and bound in Hong Kong by
Wing King Tong Co. Ltd

The drawings on pages 9 and 56 are
reproduced by kind permission of The
Consumers' Association.

## PORTRAIT OF AN ARTIST

Ray Evans has lived near Salisbury for over thirty years, but his background is Welsh and he started his artistic career in an architect's office in North Wales. During the war, while still a soldier, he spent two months at the Istituto di Belle Arti in Florence and this set him on the road to his future career.

On his return to England he studied at Manchester College of Art and then at Heatherley's School of Art in London under Iain Macnab.

After working as a freelance illustrator and cartoonist for various newspapers and magazines, including *Punch*, he returned to his first love of watercolour painting, as well as book illustration and book jacket design. This, together with teaching part-time at various art colleges, enabled him to develop his work.

He was elected a member of the Royal Institute of Painters in Watercolours in 1966, and a Fellow of the Society of Architectural Illustrators in 1979.

Ray Evans has never lost his original interest in architectural drawing and painting, but he also draws and paints landscapes and figures in landscapes. Since 1970 he has worked solely as a painter and illustrator working mainly for industry and commerce. He began writing in 1980 and this is his fifth book.

The primitive urge to create is with all of us and we are indeed fortunate if at an early age we had parents and teachers who gave us the encouragement and opportunity to express our creativity. To look at the drawings done by small children these days is very illuminating indeed. The influence of what they see on television and their sophisticated toys is obvious in their drawings and they also have the benefit of a wealth of coloured markers and pens to draw with, which I certainly didn't have at their age. I cannot remember what I drew when I was very young but I do know that I started keeping my first sketchbooks at the age of fourteen when I was given a new touring bicycle by my parents. Thus my wanderlust was born and armed with a sketchbook my travels began.

Although we lived in the north of England, I was always thinking of the land of my fathers - the hills of North Wales and the farm where I spent so much time in my childhood. My parents were keen botanists and we chugged twice a year, at Easter and summer, by steam train to Dolgellau in North Wales. Sadly, trains no longer run to or through this lovely town. As soon as I had my bicycle I used to cycle there, either on my own or with friends. I got to know every hill and landmark in the area and drew them all, too. One of the many sketches I did at this time is shown above - a hut at the top of Cadaer Idris mountain.

I took to cycling seriously and kept log books of my journeys with road profile drawings. These were illustrated with a little church here, a strange hill or mountain there, an odd-looking five-barred gate, or a humorous incident. These drawings were landmarks in more ways than one - they were my first sketchbooks and although some have been lost over the years, I still have several and refer to them even now. For the next few years my bicycle took me all over the North of England - to Wales, Cheshire, Staffordshire, Yorkshire and the Lake District, and into the hills and dales of Derbyshire, where my mother came from. On all these occasions I was armed with sketchbooks in my pocket or rucksack, and these sketching expeditions got me into the habit of observing what I was seeing - an invaluable asset for any artist. So I really recommend that you try to acquire the sketching habit - and take your sketchbook with you whenever you can.

I was lucky to have two uncles who were both artists – one an engraver with his own press, and the other a good painter who lived for a time in Paris where he met Picasso and his contemporaries in the artists' cafés of the Left Bank. I possess some of his work and he was a great influence on me. Although I wanted to go to art school, it was not a career my father thought 'safe' and so I was articled to an architect and surveyor. I worked there for eighteen months and learned a great deal about drawing. Though much of it was narrow and disciplined, it was, I believe, very useful, because I developed a knowledge and love of architecture and buildings. I learned how to measure a building and its relationship to its boundaries and then, back in the drawing office, make accurate plans and elevations of it from my notes. This was to be very useful knowledge later when I started drawing buildings freehand. It helped me to understand proportion, scale and perspective and this, together with studying building construction, resulted years later in my book *Drawing and Painting Buildings* (Collins).

## Adapting techniques to your surroundings

When the Second World War came, I enlisted in 1940 and I have included here some drawings which I did while I was serving in the army and struggling to formulate a drawing technique. It is interesting to look back and see how my style has developed from these early days. It was some time before I began to realise that technique is not the only important thing to strive for but that composition and an eye for the subject are important too. It is dangerous to become a slave to technique, because eventually with practice it will come naturally.

In the war I was assigned to a Survey Unit where we were trained to become army surveyors, and most of my particular work in action was on Observation Posts, drawing panorama of the enemy front. Two identical drawings had to be made with a grid superimposed showing compass bearings and this became excellent practice in drawing landscapes. I had grandstand views of many major and minor battle fronts in North Africa and Italy. Again, it was vital that my observation of the scene was accurate and detailed, so all the time I was learning to see with an artist's eye. It was extremely useful training.

However, throughout most of the Italian campaign (and for the eight months I spent on the North African campaign), a great proportion of the time was spent in utter boredom, occasionally interspersed with short periods of being frightened out of one's wits, so there was plenty of time to draw. I have shown here some drawings which I made while in Italy during that time and which were drawn with a pen. The Italians seemed to understand and accept my sketching activities and I was lucky enough to be able to borrow a pack mule called Vittoria and go into the hills on my own with a sketchbook.

Then, as now, I sketched whenever I had the chance, and with the added interest of new places it was extremely enjoyable, if at times a little disturbing. The drawings overleaf of the Coldstream Guard position and the village in the mountains where the Germans had their position were done during this period, as was the drawing of Vietri Bridge, Salerno, during the beach head operation in 1943. It was strange to be in

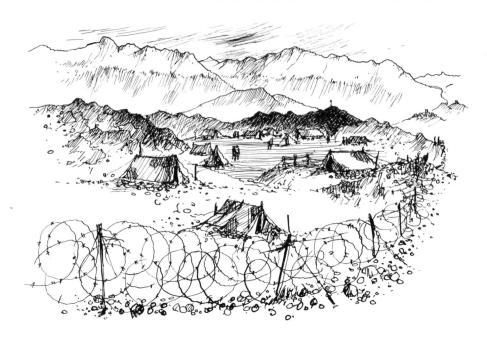

such a beautiful place in a wartime situation but, luckily, I was able to return to the area in more peaceful times while on leave. Little did I realise that forty years later I would return to sketch in the hills of Tuscany, where my son now lives with his Italian wife and their son.

This groundwork in drawing as a young soldier was sowing the seeds of my subsequent career. While still in the army, I studied at the Istituto di Belle Arti in Florence for two months and it was while I was there that a fortuitous meeting led to another great influence in my life. One day, while sketching by the Duomo Cathedral, I met an Italian professional painter called Mario Baccheli. He approached me because he saw me painting directly in watercolour without any preliminary drawing, and he thought of this as the English method of painting. I still had a lot to learn at that time and was just experimenting with a method which is

common enough but difficult as an early discipline. He turned out to be a painter of some note and we met regularly in those days at the end of the war. It is this direct method of painting that I have followed most often ever since and although I also use line with colour I tend to use line at a later stage. When painting architecture I like to use different sizes of square-ended watercolour brushes and paint directly onto the paper without any preliminary drawing. This allows for accuracy but also a free painting style. I often blot or wash out these first areas of colour until I feel that I have the proportions correct, then I can strengthen the colour and/or add line later. On occasions, however, I do reverse the process. The key is to draw freely and avoid rigidity in the strokes.

However, it must be remembered that, in a sketch or painting, my aim is not to slavishly copy what I see in front of me. I may want to change or exaggerate certain aspects – proportions, scale or perspective, colour or tone – to suit the way I see or wish to interpret the scene. For instance, in the sketch of Brixham on page 49 I somewhat elongated and narrowed the buildings rising up the hill to reinforce the height and dramatic sense I felt when I first looked at the scene. It was done almost subconsciously. A mere photographic interpretation could not do justice to my feeling about the place.

On my return to England I went to Art College. I was among other ex-service students and we all worked extra hard to make up for the lost war years, but in my case, at least I had had the good fortune to see all those wonderful Italian cities and to have been inspired by them. Cities have been my happiest hunting grounds ever since, and for me sketching in London and other great cities, like New York, Rome and Leningrad, to

name just a few, is the richest of occupations. There is something to inspire you at every corner and usually a place to sit where you are hardly noticed if you don't like attention, although the attention you do get is often of the friendliest kind.

With the start of spring and sunny days in early March, my enjoyment really begins and, even if I am busy on painting commissions, I always go outside to sketch for an hour if it is a nice day. This does not mean that I don't sketch in the winter, but I find that the feeling of spring in the air is irresistible. Whatever season you prefer, I think it's a good idea to make an effort to sketch outdoor scenes all year round. If you can't face sitting outside in the winter chill, you can always sketch through a window, or from the car.

If I am close to home I carry at least three sizes of sketchbook since I never know what size page a subject will be likely to need. Recently, on a Sunday morning in Salisbury when there were not many people about, I used a larger-sized sketchbook and took three-and-a-half hours on the subject: a street scene that needed a lot of time. On my return home I tore the page out and stretched it on a board using adhesive Gum strip because I wanted to work on it further.

Many people ask when is a sketch not a sketch? Or, when does it become a painting, or even, does this distinction matter? Sometimes the merest sketch, well mounted and framed, becomes the most desired piece of work in an exhibition. Yet the difference is there – a painting is a piece of work that has been carried out with planning and forethought and usually from sketches made on the spot. While a sketch is a spontaneous, immediate interpretation of the subject in front of you, usually done in a limited time. I find that my best sketches are made quickly in just sixty to ninety minutes.

**Use your sketches as memory aids**

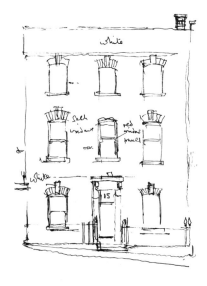

If you are sketching a subject you think would make a larger or more finished painting than is feasible to paint on the spot, don't hesitate to make notes on your sketches with any information that you think will be useful and relevant. Make notes in the margin, using lines and arrows to help you to remember colours, tone values and even actual measurements. Most important is the direction of the light source and I find it useful always to record the date, place and time of day. The weather could also be a useful point to note. Make several sketches from different angles, and some compositional sketches of how you think the picture should be composed.

Don't hesitate to use a camera for reference – not to copy from but perhaps for close-ups of the subject, or details of brick or stonework. The camera has been used as an aid by artists for over a hundred years – indeed the Impressionists used cameras, although obviously their references were in black and white. Black and white photographs are useful as reference when used in conjunction with a sketch because at least the tone values are more correct than in a colour print. Much colour printing is innaccurate, although colour slides do show colours more accurately than prints, and if projected onto a wall or large screen they can be sketched from in a more realistic way. Unless you are a very experienced

artist, try not to copy directly from a photograph as you will be disappointed with the results if you do. A photograph is inevitably flat and might be affected by paralex (distortion). In any case, your own composition can be made much more interesting than any photograph on the subject. However, by all means take colour slides of your own work and file these for future reference or for lectures.

I once went on a lecture tour to the USA and the architectural students there were very keen for me to give them drawing and painting demonstrations. I was surprised at their lack of ability to draw convincing freehand sketches when they could turn out beautifully drawn plans, elevations and mechanical perspectives. There were exceptions of course, and I have some architect friends who are fine artists in their own right, but there are many who would admit to not being able to draw freehand at all well.

However, it is not just a question of being able to draw. Equally important when sketching is the composition of the picture – where to place the horizon and how to make the subject as interesting as possible. A horizon across the middle of the page is aesthetically unpleasing so you have to decide whether to put it high or low. I often prefer a high horizon because I like interesting foregrounds where the eye can easily be led into the picture. But if there is an interesting sky with perhaps massive cloud shapes, or there are high mountains or tall spires and buildings above the horizon, then a low horizon will suit the composition better. I have shown here a sketch where the high horizon leads the eye down the page. Another good example is on page 40 – a snow scene sketched from my bedroom window with watercolours in a cartridge paper sketchbook. I placed the horizon at the top of the page where an interesting pattern of trees and hills dropped down across a snow field and led to a hedge and gate in the foreground at the bottom of the page.

But while the ability to draw and the necessity to make your sketch visually interesting should not be overlooked, an important ingredient for the successful sketch is the excitement of a subject which suddenly appeals. It is the joy of an unexpected scene or event that I find most stimulating when sketching. I am always searching for new and exciting subjects and if you look around you with an artist's eye there are probably some good compositions in your own backyard. I have a painter colleague with whom I taught many years ago, who used to paint his small garden in all different sorts of weather and these paintings were all gems. Living things in the garden are constantly changing – the buds you sketched yesterday are today flowers, the tree in full leaf is now just a skeleton. Birds, too, often provide interesting subjects for your sketches. It is a simple matter to spend a few minutes each day in your own back garden to practise different techniques, or try out different materials.

## Take advantage of unexpected situations

If you are dissatisfied with your sketches, perhaps you are not approaching sketching in the right frame of mind. Enjoyment of the scene comes first, but try to look around you with a fresh eye and see familiar scenes differently. Learn to take advantage of the weather or the unexpected situation. The other morning I was awakened by a cock pheasant making distress calls. It was early, before seven o'clock, and as I looked out of the window the pheasant was walking down our drive, clucking sadly. He went across the road and stood in the field still clucking. My wife went out in the car later and, by the roadside near our house, found a dead hen pheasant which had obviously been hit by a car. I picked up the dead bird, laid her on newspaper in the studio and spent the morning making this pencil and wash drawing of her. Unlucky for

the cock pheasant, who still wandered near the house many days later, but it is an ill wind, as the saying goes, and I made use of the accident.

Always familiarise yourself with the subject first before you begin to sketch. When you have finally decided where you are going to work from, there are still one or two practical points to consider. For example, if you are working outside, is the sun likely to be shining right in your face before long and thus make the subject difficult to see? Is there the possibility that someone will park their car in front of your view? Will you be obstructing the pavement or doorway where you are sitting? When in doubt about whether you should be in a particular place at all, do ask. Invariably, people are kind to artists and will give permission.

As I have already said, you should find a subject that really interests you, especially if you wish to try out a new method or technique. Your particular interest might lie in botanical drawings, flowers or people, and we are all usually led in some direction or other. My own early train-

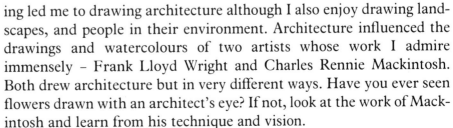

ing led me to drawing architecture although I also enjoy drawing landscapes, and people in their environment. Architecture influenced the drawings and watercolours of two artists whose work I admire immensely – Frank Lloyd Wright and Charles Rennie Mackintosh. Both drew architecture but in very different ways. Have you ever seen flowers drawn with an architect's eye? If not, look at the work of Mackintosh and learn from his technique and vision.

**Sketchbooks are ideal for trying new techniques**

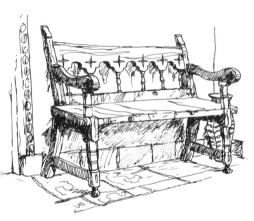

**Use any spare time to practise sketching**

When you have time, or are unable to go out sketching because of the weather, the comfort of your home is the ideal place to experiment with new techniques. Try splattering colour with a toothbrush, or even with your fingers, in half dry work. Use a hair dryer on certain areas to speed drying. Try using oil crayons, wax or varnish as a resist. Use as your subjects various fruits which have been cut into segments or sections. Sliced Kiwi fruit or red or green peppers are excellent subjects to practice various techniques. Sketch these objects in your sketchbooks using all the methods you would use on an outside subject, but also try masking out agents such as masking fluid and masking film, blotting out with tissues and white blotting paper, and washing out. Invent your own methods and you will be surprised at the effects you can get. Then you can decide which of these you can practically use when out sketching.

The subject itself will dictate to some extent the drawing method you will use, whether it is a building, a seascape or a landscape. It helps if the atmosphere is unusual, perhaps an exciting sky, for instance. A black thunder cloud behind some white cottages, which reverses the normal situation where the sky is usually the lightest part of the picture, could be an interesting composition.

However, the joy of sketching is that there are no rules to be obeyed. Use coloured paper, gouache white or Chinese white; scratch out with a sharp knife – sometimes this is very effective with water. Mask out, if you like, although I find this too cumbersome while sketching. Use a conté crayon or even a charcoal pencil together with watercolour which can be a very effective method.

A good maxim to follow as an artist is always to be prepared. I was in London recently seeing a client and this necessitated carrying a large portfolio, heavy with books and reproductions of artwork. I remembered to put in a small watercolour sketchbook measuring 6 × 6 in (150 × 150 mm), a tiny watercolour box, a 3 in (80 mm) brush and a 1 in (25 mm) Rotring stylo pen. On the way home I had an hour to wait for a train so I walked to the Embankment and, in half an hour, made a watercolour sketch of the Houses of Parliament and Big Ben in my small sketchbook, and added some coloured conté crayon to the watercolours. I think it made quite a pleasant sketch and if I hadn't been prepared for sketching, even on this busy day, I couldn't have done it.

Back home the following day there was a light covering of snow on the ground, and as I looked out of an upstairs window I saw that the snow had etched the dark lines that a tractor had made on the hillside so that they showed up as grey lines against the white, and there was a scattering of rooks and gulls feeding in the tracks. I still had my small watercolour box in my portfolio so I pulled out the box and made a quick half-hour sketch, again illustrating the importance of being able to take advantage of the odd moment when inspiration is there.

I have a friend, a good amateur artist, who used to take an earlier train to his London office so that he could have a little time to sketch his favourite buildings on the walk to the office. So there is always time for sketching and even if there seems not to be, then try to find the time.

**Try not to over-burden
yourself with equipment**

We should remember that all Turner needed to produce the most exquisite sketches was a pencil stub and a box of watercolours, and he was on foot or using a horse for transport.

However, although the most effective drawings can sometimes be done on the back of an old envelope with a fountain pen or a pencil stub, do try to use the best materials you can afford. The word sketching implies that a minimum of equipment should be carried, but that minimum must include enough to ring the changes that make sketching an exciting and interesting hobby. However, try not to overburden yourself with too much equipment. Travelling abroad as I often do, I have learned to scale down what I carry but one should remember that there may be little chance of finding replacements for your equipment. The traveller's motto is to 'take half the clothes you think you will need and twice as much money' – the travelling painter should substitute 'equipment' for clothes.

My sketchbag (illustrated here) is firmly made so that I can open it and see the contents without it collapsing. It can be used as a shoulder bag, carried by its top handle, or used as a rucksack by reclipping the straps. When I went to Morocco I knew I would be walking a good deal of the time, so I weighed my sketchbag and found that it was too heavy

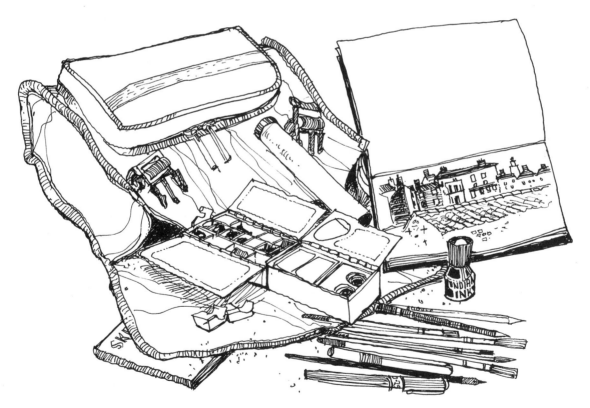

with all my kit. So I pared it down to only two sketchbooks – a pocket one and a hardback sketchbook measuring 9½ × 8 in (240 × 200 mm) which contained Heritage 400 gsm watercolour paper. I took a small watercolour box with eight colours, a few watercolour brushes mostly of the square-ended variety, some pencils, two stylo pens well cleaned and fully charged with ink, a Rotring fountain pen with black non-water-proof ink, a cloth and a small knife. This travelling kit proved adequate

13

on that occasion – I came home with a very full sketchbook and some of the results are shown in this book.

It's interesting and useful to experiment with different materials; try drawing with quill pens, and with dip pens, and not only with ink, but also with watercolours. Use the pointed end of your brush, or even a stick, to draw with and draw and paint on different coloured and textured surfaces – brown wrapping paper is very interesting to draw on.

I personally prefer hardback sketchbooks because they do tend to wear better and have to survive a lot of carrying about. Also, I like the real book 'feel' of them, rather than the spiral-bound variety. I sometimes take an additional sketchbook that I make up myself, or have made up, with different coloured paper, so that I can use gouache which is ideal on coloured paper because, unlike transparent watercolour, you can paint light into dark. A tube of Chinese white will convert your watercolours to gouache which is perfect for sketching purposes.

It is also useful to carry some felt-tipped pens, and if I feel I have room I also carry some watercolour pencils, such as those I used on the Lucca sketch on page 46. As boxes of crayons tend to be bulky and heavy, carry some in a tube similar to the one for brushes shown in the sketch on page 13. I recommend that you use the stronger and brighter watercolour pencil colours as some of the earth and pastel colours tend to lack strength. There are many other media that I have not mentioned, such as pastel or charcoal, which are all excellent for sketching.

**Draw the same subject in different media**

When I was in Tuscany recently I took a set of felt-tipped pens, as well as watercolours and crayons. One of the drawings illustrated here is of San Gimignano and I also sketched it in colour; San Gimignano is an impressive place and I thought the rather heavy and strong colours of felt-tipped pens would suit the subject. I used Tombo pens which have a fine point at one end and a brush point for broader strokes at the other end. I used a stylo pen for details of bricks, paving stones and lettering. The finished sketch is on page 47.

**The subject will often suggest the medium**

Another sketch where I felt inspired was the one I did of the view from the Torre Guinigi in Lucca, shown here in black and white and in colour on page 46. This time I felt that the subject warranted watercolour pencils. Because of the height of the tower, I was looking down over the roofs of the town, with tall houses and tall towers in the distance, and everything seemed vertical. I drew strongly in line with largely downward strokes and with the crayons kept very sharp. I also made a further drawing of the same subject using felt-tipped pens because I wanted to make a larger painting of it back in my studio and needed as much information as I could get.

This is when felt-tipped pens are most useful – for making quick compositional sketches as preliminary notes on the spot before painting a more finished watercolour later, either on the site or in the studio. Some such drawings are illustrated on pages 45 and 46.

Where tone is particularly important I use a pencil to make studies and some of these sketches are illustrated here. In particular, look at the drawing of the coast near Mojacar in Almería. I used 4B and 2B pencils and you can see how I have delineated the receding mountains running down to the sea. Although generally the darkest darks and the lightest lights are in the foreground nearest to you, a shadow cast by a cloud can sometimes reverse the process, as in this drawing.

**Use your sketchbooks to monitor your progress**

I cannot emphasize too strongly the usefulness and importance of a sketchbook and also the sheer joy of using one, and the best advice I can give to aspiring artists at whatever level is to fix the sketchbook habit into your lifestyle. I firmly believe that the more practice you have at sketching the better you become. Equip yourself with a number of

sketchbooks of different sizes and different types of paper. Date each page and note the time and place of the sketch. Don't destroy pages where you feel the sketch is a failure, but try to learn by your mistakes. Never use an eraser, but correct a wrong stroke by drawing over it. You will find that you gain confidence by drawing directly with a pen or with colour without a pre-drawn guide line. But don't just practise in a mind-less way – drawing is an intellectual process and you should continually be looking critically at your own work. This is why you should date your sketchbooks so that you can compare them with earlier or later work. When you have mastered an attractive new technique, try not to slav-ishly repeat it in all your drawings. Look at other artists' work and try to analyse their methods and techniques.

We are all inspired by others; hopefully we do not copy them, but studying a good artist's work is very useful and thought-provoking. Skill is important but originality is just as essential, although I do not mean that you should draw in a way that is unnatural for you. You should always try to put something of yourself into your work and not just copy someone else's method and style.

The most significant way to do this is to try to be original with your composition or picture making. Look at your subject with new eyes and you will be surprised how interesting you can make the most familiar scene by changing the way you look at it. A view through a window may be more interesting if the window is half shut, or the view only occupies a quarter of your picture. Also, try *thinking* a little differently about what you see. If you look at the pencil drawing here of the fishing lofts at Hastings and then at the felt-tipped pen drawing in colour on page 45 of a view looking between two of the huts perhaps you can see how I was searching for a new or different view of them.

## The value of sketching with other artists

My insatiable habit of sketching has been the key to my life; through all the difficult times I have experienced I have continued to draw and my drawing has flourished. The itch to get out my pen or pencil when sitting in a café, when travelling abroad, or on a local train to London, is always with me. But what is it that inspires me? This question has intrigued me for years and I think the answer lies in the spark of creativity which is within each of us – for me the outlet is in drawing.

Once a year I always try to get together with several of my friends and we run a 'Sketching Workshop' by invitation to twelve or more artists. The object is to sketch all day and then, in the evening, to discuss in the studio the work we have done. During the week we show the small paintings we have each brought with us, and then at the end of the week we have an exhibition of our completed work. We learn a lot from each other; some of us are inveterate travellers and all of us are inveterate sketchers, and so it is exciting to look through each others' sketchbooks. This is also the value of taking a sketching or painting holiday, or sketching with friends. It will enable you to compare notes with other artists and there is a great sense of comradeship which adds to the joy of sketching and in turn stimulates one's work.

A sketchbook is a very personal thing and none of the sketches illustrated on these pages was carried out with this book in mind as the sole purpose of the work. I approach each subject by concentrating only on what I am creating or trying to create on the page, and I hope that you will, too. There can be little more satisfying to an artist than having a row of sketchbooks on the shelf; they become illustrated diaries of your life.

Be hungry for subjects that you can fill your sketchbooks with, wherever in the world you may be. Not only will they develop your skills as an artist and record your progress, but they will serve as a lasting image of places visited and people you have met. My sketchbooks are the most important books I will ever own and something that no money can buy – so I urge you never to be without one, or even several, in constant use.

*I sketched this view of a hillside in Mojacar, Spain, using pencils. When working with soft pencils always draw from the top of the page downwards to avoid smudging.*

*Both these sketches, winter scenes in Yorkshire, were drawn with 2B and 4B pencils.*

OPPOSITE: *I used a felt-tipped pen for this sketch of a barn near Salisbury. It illustrates well how effective economy of line can be, in particular the tyre tread of a tractor along the path.*

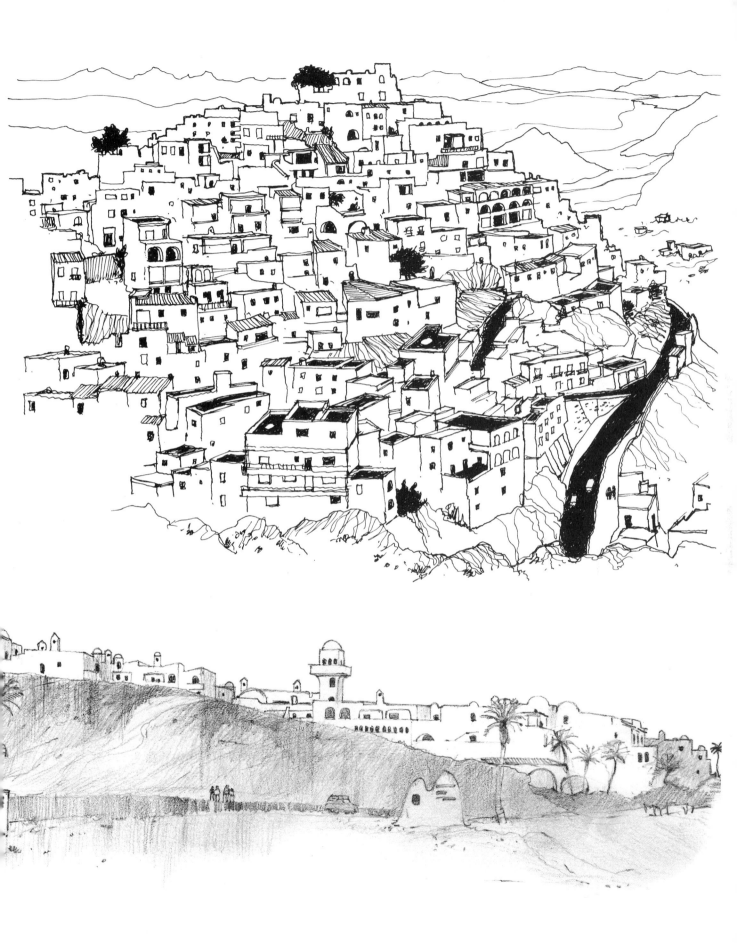

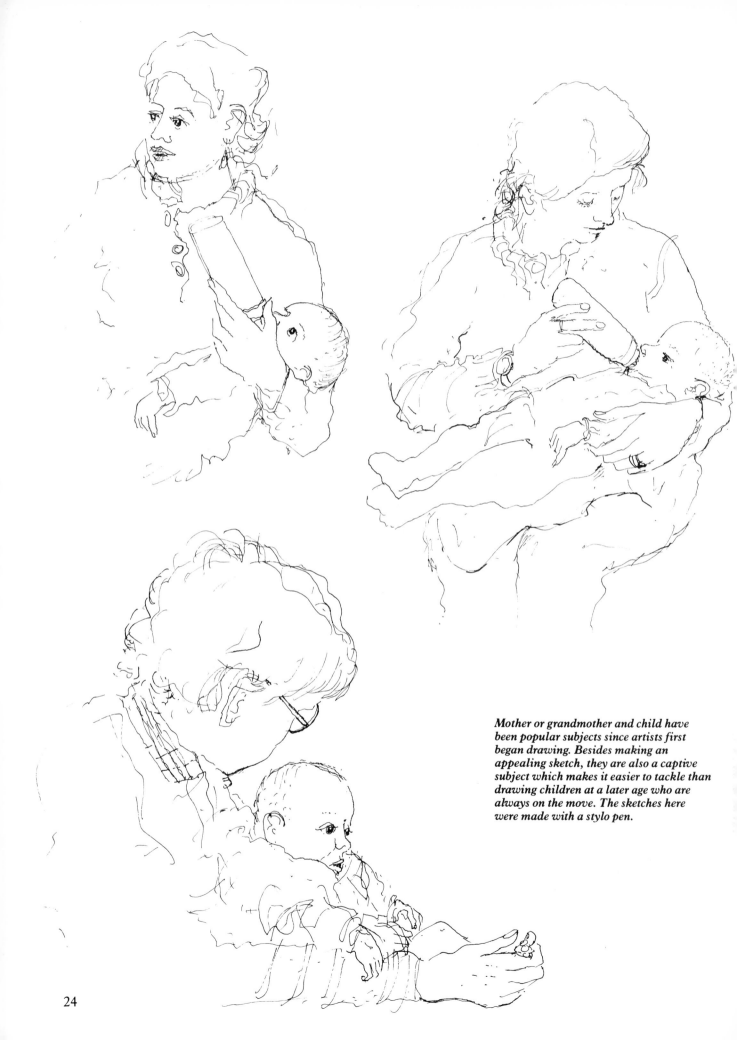

*Mother or grandmother and child have been popular subjects since artists first began drawing. Besides making an appealing sketch, they are also a captive subject which makes it easier to tackle than drawing children at a later age who are always on the move. The sketches here were made with a stylo pen.*

These fountain pen drawings were made on a train. Whether the baby is asleep or dozily awake, I always begin with the difficult parts – the face and hands, because if the infant changes position the shape of the rest of its body doesn't alter very much.

*These characters were all drawn on trains where, more often than not, my subjects were either asleep, reading or working. I do not think these people were aware that I was sketching them as I am fairly adept at appearing to look elsewhere, or even seeming to be sketching someone else.*

31

Small children are a delight to draw. You have to work quickly as they tend to move around a lot, but treat your sketches of them just as sketch notes. These were drawn with felt-tipped pens having a fine point at one end and a soft, broader point at the other.

*I sketched this lunch party (above) while in a pub. I used a stylo pen, then surreptitiously added a little colour using a very small watercolour box under the edge of the table.*
*I made a drawing of each character first and added the colour when they were all completed.*

*This sketch, of Carnarfon Castle, was done very quickly – in about 12 minutes. I used a watercolour wash first and then added line.* OPPOSITE: *Another quick sketch done in the same way, this is Wilton House, Salisbury.*

ROSTERANS

Ray Evans

These two quick sketches were made using pen and wash, and, in addition, I used felt-tipped pens on the lower one. I liked the interesting shapes made against the sky by both the pier and the boats' masts.

HUSS
COD
SKATE
PLAICE
LEMON SOLE
DOVER SOLE
CRABS
& PRAWNS

MUSSELS
COCKLES
DRESSED
CRAB

Hastings.

*This sketch was drawn with watercolour pencils from the top of Torre Guinigi in Lucca; there is a pen and ink drawing of the same subject at the top of page 15.* OPPOSITE: *I used felt-tipped and stylo pens for this sketch of San Gimignano; there is a pen and wash drawing of a different view on page 14.*

*I find the wide variety of roofs one sees very interesting, and they are ideal as references for use in larger paintings. The addition of birds, aerials and scaffolding adds an extra dimension to the sketches.*

*Trees have always fascinated me and these three sketches
are interesting because I have used different techniques to
show the contrast between different types of tree. I am
particularly intrigued by the pattern that trees make both
in winter and in summer, and the drawing above
demonstrates this.*

53

*I couldn't resist this subject – a cycle race by Lake Geneva at Lausanne. I had meant to paint a watercolour of the town but when these cyclists arrived I changed my mind and sketched them instead. The atmosphere was very lively with constant movement. I took about 40 minutes on the sketch.*

These pen drawings of Italy were actually
sketched from photographic references. If you
have only a photograph to use as reference, it
is better to draw in strong line, as shown here,
rather than make a painting directly from the
photograph. Use your imagination,
eliminating unnecessary detail or changing
relevant aspects, to make an interesting
picture.

*These contrasting drawings, both of boats, are an example of the very quick sketch (above),*
*and the more considered drawing taking perhaps an hour or more (below).*

ABOVE: *A pen and wash sketch of Corris, North Wales.* LEFT: *Another pen and wash, this time of the grounds around Wilton House, near Salisbury. I was attracted by the giant fir trees and the shadows they cast.*

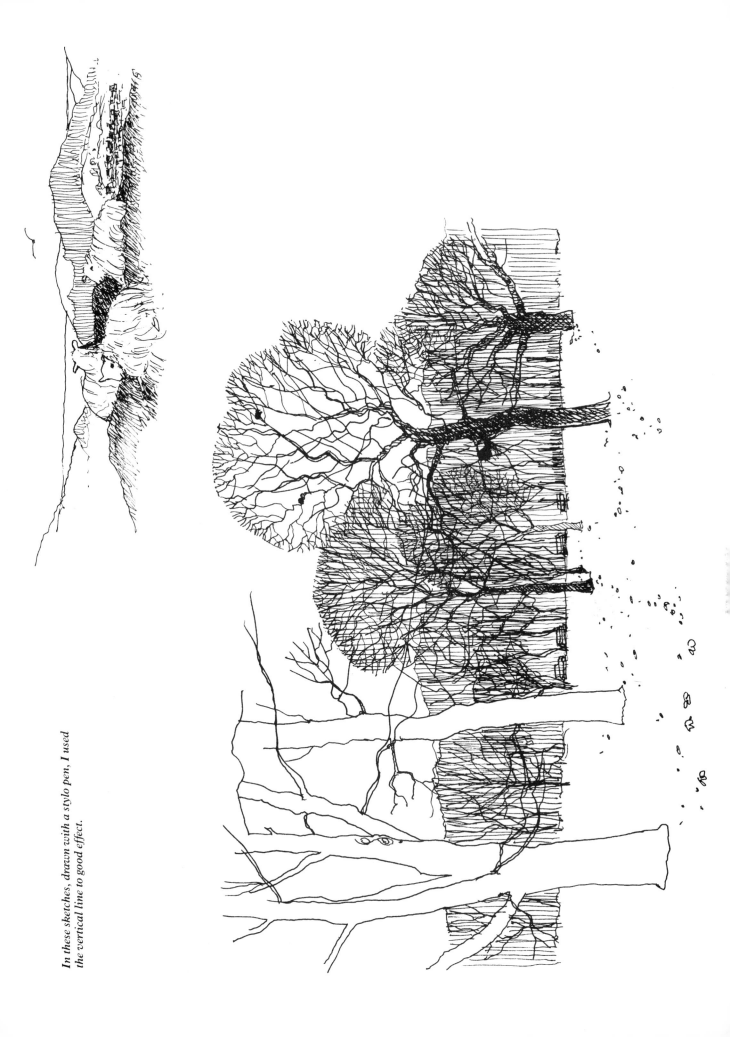

*In these sketches, drawn with a stylo pen, I used
the vertical line to good effect.*

*These are sketches made during a concert given by Russian musicians. I often sketch at concerts, particularly when the orchestra is tuning up. Here I used a stylo pen and a fountain pen.*